YOU'RE THE CHEF

DANDY Desserts

Kari Cornell Photographs by Brie Cohen

MILLBROOK PRESS • MINNEAPOLIS

For my mom, who taught me how to experiment in the kitchen;
and for Will, Theo, and Brian, who cheerfully sampled
every dessert I put on the table —K.C.

For Kate and Dick Vlach and their wonderful desserts —B.C.

Photography by Brie Cohen
Food in photographs prepared by chef David Vlach
Illustrations by Laura Westlund/Independent Picture Service
The image on page 5 is used with the permission of © iStockphoto.com/stuartbur.

Millbrook Press
A division of Lerner Publishing Group, Inc.
241 First Avenue North
Minneapolis, MN 55401 U.S.A.

Website address: www.lernerbooks.com

Main body text set in Felbridge Std Regular 11/14.
Typeface provided by Monotype Typography.

Library of Congress Cataloging-in-Publication Data

Cornell, Kari A.
Dandy desserts /
by Kari Cornell ; photographs by Brie Cohen.
pages   cm. — (You're the chef)
Includes index.
ISBN 978–0–7613–6644–7 (lib. bdg. : alk. paper)
ISBN 978–1–4677–1718–2 (eBook)
1. Desserts—Juvenile literature. I. Cohen, Brie, illustrator. II. Title.
TX773.C634434 2014
641.86—dc23   2012048924

Manufactured in the United States of America
1 – CG – 7/15/13

TABLE of CONTENTS

Are you ready to make some delightfully dandy desserts?
YOU can be the chef and make food for yourself and your family.
These easy recipes are perfect for a chef who is just learning to cook.
And they're so delicious, you'll want to make them again and again!

I developed these recipes with the help of my kids, who are six and
eight years old. They can't do all the cooking on their own yet, but
they can do a lot.

Can't get enough of cooking? Check out www.lerneresource.com
for bonus recipes, healthful eating tips, links to cooking technique
videos, and more!

BEFORE YOU START

Reserve your space! Always ask for permission to work in the kitchen.

Find a helper! You will need an adult helper for some tasks. Talk with this
person to decide what steps you can do on your own and what steps the adult
will help with.

Make a plan! Read through the whole recipe before you start cooking.
Do you have the ingredients you'll need? If you don't know what a certain
ingredient is, see page 31 to find out more. Do you understand each step? If
you don't understand a technique, such as *mix* or *thaw*, turn to page 7. At the
beginning of each recipe, you'll see how much time you'll need to prepare the
recipe and to cook it. The recipe will also tell you how many servings it makes.
Small drawings at the top of each recipe let you know what major kitchen
equipment you'll need—such as a stovetop, a mixer, or a microwave.

stovetop

electric mixer

knives

microwave

oven

Wash up! Always wash your hands with soap and water before you start cooking. And wash them again after you touch raw eggs, meat, or fish.

Get it together! Find the tools you'll use, such as measuring cups or a mixing bowl. Gather all the ingredients you'll need. That way you won't have to stop to look for things once you start cooking.

SAFETY TIPS

That's sharp! Your adult helper needs to be in the kitchen when you are using a knife, a grater, or a peeler. If you are doing the cutting, use a cutting board. Cut away from your body, and keep your fingers away from the blade.

That's hot! Be sure an adult is in the kitchen if you use the stove or the oven. Your adult helper can help you cook on the stove and take hot things out of the oven.

Tie it back! If you have long hair, tie it back or wear a hat. If you have long sleeves, roll them up. You want to keep your hair and clothing out of the food and away from flames or other heat sources.

Turn that handle! When cooking on the stove, turn the pot handle toward the back. That way, no one will accidentally bump the pot and knock it off the stove.

Wash it! If you are working with raw eggs or meat, you need to keep things extra clean. After cutting raw meat or fish, wash the knife and the cutting board right away. They must be clean before you use them to cut anything else.

Go slowly! Take your time when you're working. When you are doing something for the first time, such as peeling or grating, be sure not to rush.

Above all, have fun!

Finish the job right!

One of your most important jobs as a chef is to clean up when you're done. Wash the dishes with soap and warm water. Wipe off the countertop or the table. Put away any unused ingredients. The adults in your house will be more excited for you to cook next time if you take charge of cleaning up.

COOKING TOOLS

baking pans

bowls

can opener

colander

cookie sheet

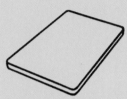
cutting board

dry measuring cups

electric mixer

knives

ladle

liquid measuring cup

loaf pan

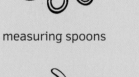
measuring spoons

muffin tin

pie pan

rolling pins

rubber scraper

saucepans

serrated knife

spatula

table knife

vegetable peeler

whisk

wire cooling rack

wooden spoon

TECHNIQUES

bake: to cook in the oven

blend: to use an electric mixer or a spoon to stir ingredients together until well mixed

boil: to heat liquid on a stovetop until the liquid starts to bubble

chill: to place a food in the refrigerator to make it cold

chop: to cut food into small pieces using a knife

coat: to cover food with another ingredient, such as sugar or oil

discard: to throw away or put in a compost bin. Discarded parts of fruits and vegetables and eggshells can be put in a compost bin, if you have one.

grease: to coat a pan in oil or butter so baked food won't stick to the bottom

mix: to stir food using a spoon or a fork

preheat: to turn the oven to the temperature you will need for baking. An oven takes about 15 minutes to heat up.

serrated: a tool, such as a knife, that has a bumpy edge

set aside: to put nearby in a bowl or a plate or on a clean workspace

slice: to cut food into thin pieces

soften: to remove butter or cream cheese from the refrigerator so it warms up and becomes soft

sprinkle: to scatter on top

thaw: to warm up frozen food until it is soft

whisk: to stir or whip with a whisk or a fork

MEASURING

To measure dry ingredients, such as sugar or flour, spoon the ingredient into a measuring cup until it is full. Then use the back of a table knife to level it off. Do not pack it down unless the recipe tells you to. Do not use measuring cups made for liquids.

When you're measuring a **liquid**, such as milk or water, use a clear glass or plastic measuring cup. Set the cup on the table or a counter and pour the liquid into the cup. Pour slowly and stop when the liquid has reached the correct line.

Don't measure your ingredients over the bowl they will go into. If you accidentally spill, you might have way too much!

makes 24 cupcakes

preparation time: 25 minutes
baking time: 15 to 20 minutes

ingredients:

8 ounces cream cheese
¾ cup (1½ sticks) unsalted butter
1 (15.25-ounce) box cake mix, any
   flavor
1 cup water
½ cup canola oil
3 eggs
2 cups powdered sugar
1 teaspoon vanilla extract
colored decorator sugars or
   sprinkles
small round candies, such as Red
   Hots or jelly beans
black string licorice

equipment:

24 muffin tin liners
1 to 4 muffin tins
large mixing bowl
liquid measuring cup
electric mixer
rubber scraper
ladle
oven mitts
toothpicks
wire cooling rack
medium mixing bowl
measuring cup—1 cup
measuring spoons
table knife

Critter Cupcakes

Make these fun cupcakes for a birthday treat or Halloween.
Create colorful critters on top with licorice and sprinkles.
Or use your favorite candies for decoration!

1. **Remove** the cream cheese and butter from the refrigerator, so they have time to soften.

2. **Preheat** the oven to 325°F.

3. **Place** muffin tin liners into muffin tins.

4. In a large mixing bowl, **combine** the cake mix, water, canola oil, and eggs. **Mix** with an electric mixer on medium speed for 2 minutes. Wash the mixer's beaters and set aside.

5. Use a ladle to **scoop** the batter into the prepared muffin cups. **Fill** each cup two-thirds full.

6. Use oven mitts to **place** the muffin tins into the oven. **Bake** for 15 to 20 minutes, or until done. To check for doneness, use oven mitts to **remove** a muffin tin. Stick a toothpick into the center of a cupcake. If the toothpick comes out clean, the cupcakes are done. If pieces of cupcake cling to the toothpick, bake the cupcakes for 2 to 3 more minutes. Then test them again. Repeat as needed.

Turn the page for more Critter Cupcakes

Critter Cupcakes continued

7. Use oven mitts to **remove** the cupcakes from the oven. Allow to **cool** on a wire cooling rack for 2 minutes. Then use a fork to **lift** each cupcake from the muffin tin and **place** it onto the cooling rack. Cool for about 20 minutes, or until completely cool.

8. Make the frosting while the cupcakes cool. **Place** the softened cream cheese, butter, powdered sugar, and vanilla extract into the medium mixing bowl. Use the electric mixer to **mix** well.

9. Frost the cupcakes once they are cool. Use a table knife to **spread** frosting on each of the cupcakes.

10. **Make** a critter on top of each cupcake. Use the colored sugar, sprinkles, round candies, and licorice to **create** bees, ladybugs, turtles, or spiders. Or design a critter of your own! Serve immediately so the decorations look their best.

TRY THIS!

Make colored frosting for your cupcakes. Scoop ½ cup of the frosting into a small bowl. Add 1 to 2 drops of a food coloring of your choice. (It doesn't take much!) Mix well with a spoon.

To save time, use 2 cans of white, ready-made frosting from the store.

Favorite Ice Cream Pie

Choose your favorite ice cream flavor to make
this cool and creamy treat.

1. **Thaw** ice cream in the refrigerator for 1 to 1½
   hours, or until quite soft. Remove the whipped
   topping from the freezer to **thaw** in the kitchen.

2. Use a rubber scraper to **scrape**
   the soft ice cream into the
   graham cracker crust. Use the
   rubber scraper to **spread** the
   ice cream until it is smooth.

3. **Cover** the pie with a piece of plastic wrap,
   and **place** in the freezer for 1 hour.

4. **Remove** the ice cream
   pie from the freezer.
   Spread whipped topping
   evenly over the top of
   the pie. **Sprinkle** with
   cinnamon. Then **slice** the
   pie into pieces, and serve
   immediately.

serves 8

preparation time: 5 minutes
thawing time: 1½ hours
freezing time: 1 hour
baking time: 0

ingredients:
1 pint ice cream, any flavor
1 (8-ounce) tub whipped
topping, such as Cool
Whip, thawed
1 (6-ounce) ready-made
graham cracker crust
¼ teaspoon cinnamon

equipment:
rubber scraper
plastic wrap
measuring spoons
knife

makes 8 turnovers

thawing time: overnight
preparation time: 20 minutes
baking time: 25 minutes

ingredients:

1 (17-ounce) package frozen puff
   pastry
1 (21-ounce) can cherry pie filling
¼ cup all-purpose flour
1 tablespoon coarse sugar
   (optional)

equipment:

cookie sheet
can opener
small bowl
measuring cup—¼ cup
rolling pin
table knife
measuring spoons
oven mitts
pastry brush

Flaky Cherry Turnovers

These turnovers are like individual cherry pies
but more fun to make!

1. **Place** the frozen puff pastry in the
   refrigerator to thaw overnight.

2. When you are ready to begin baking,
   preheat the oven to 350°F.

3. **Open** the cherry pie filling with a can opener,
   and **fill** a small bowl with water. Place both
   near your work area. Then sprinkle the flour
   on your clean work surface.

4. **Unwrap** the first sheet of puff pastry on the floured
   area. Use a rolling pin to **flatten** fold creases and
   close up holes along the fold lines.

5. Use a table knife to **cut** the sheet into 4 equal squares.

6. **Place** the squares on an ungreased cookie sheet about 1 inch apart. The pastry squares should be positioned like diamonds. Repeat with the second sheet of puff pastry.

Turn the page for more Flaky Cherry Turnovers

TRY THIS!

Replace cherry pie filling with **apple pie filling.**

Make the filling with fresh **peaches, pears, apples, or blueberries.** Mix 2 cups chopped fruit with ¼ cup sugar, 2 tablespoons flour, and ½ teaspoon cinnamon.

Serve the turnovers with a scoop of vanilla ice cream.
Yum!

Flaky Cherry Turnovers continued

7. **Place** 1½ tablespoons of cherry filling in the center of the diamond. **Dip** your finger in the water bowl. Then run your finger along the edges of a diamond to wet the edges slightly.

8. **Lift** one corner of the diamond. **Fold** it over the opposite corner to form a triangle. With a fork, **press** together the edges of the pastry to seal in the filling. Then use a table knife to **cut** a 2-inch slit on top of the turnover. **Repeat** steps 7 and 8 with the remaining squares.

9. If you are using coarse sugar, dip a pastry brush in the water bowl. **Brush** a very small amount of water across the top of each turnover. Sprinkle the sugar on each turnover.

10. Use oven mitts to **place** the cookie sheets in the oven. **Bake** for 25 minutes, or until golden brown. Allow to cool completely on cookie sheets before eating—the filling will be hot!

Instant Chocolate Cake

Looking for a quick dessert that will impress your family? This is the one! These individual cakes "bake" in the microwave, so they are ready to serve in minutes.

serves 1

preparation time: 5 minutes
cooking time: 3 minutes

ingredients:
1 tablespoons flour
4 tablespoons sugar
3 tablespoons cocoa powder
¼ teaspoon cinnamon
3 tablespoons chocolate chips
3 tablespoons warm water
3 tablespoons oil
½ teaspoon vanilla extract
½ teaspoon white vinegar

equipment:
1 (12-ounce) microwave-safe
coffee mug
measuring spoons
fork
oven mitts

1. **Add** all the ingredients to the coffee mug. **Stir** with a fork to mix well.

2. **Place** the mug in the microwave, and **cook** on high for 3 minutes. Use oven mitts to **remove** the hot mug from the microwave. Allow to cool for 1 to 2 minutes before eating.

3. To make more than one serving, **repeat** steps 1 and 2 for each cake.

TRY THIS!
Leave out the cinnamon, and replace the chocolate chips with peanut butter chips.

Add 1½ tablespoons chopped walnuts in step 1.

15

serves 6 to 8

preparation time: 20 minutes
baking time: 10 to 15 minutes
chilling time: 1 hour

ingredients:

1 (12-ounce) tub whipped
   topping, such as Cool Whip,
   thawed
1 (8-inch) frozen, premade
   piecrust
1 (4-ounce) package instant
   banana cream pudding
1¾ cups cold milk
3 medium ripe bananas

equipment:

pie pan
fork
oven mitts
medium mixing bowl
liquid measuring cup
whisk
table knife
cutting board
rubber scraper

Banana Cream Pie

Nothing tastes better than a banana cream pie on a warm summer day. For best flavor, make this recipe when you have bananas that are just beginning to get a few brown spots.

1. **Remove** the whipped topping from the freezer so it has time to thaw. **Remove** the piecrust from the freezer 15 to 20 minutes before you are ready to begin baking.

2. **Preheat** the oven to 400°F.

3. Carefully **place** the thawed crust in a pie pan. Use a fork to **poke** tiny holes all over the bottom of the piecrust.

4. Use oven mitts to **place** the piecrust in the oven. Bake for 10 to 15 minutes, or until light brown. Do not overbake the crust. Use oven mitts to **remove** the crust from the oven. Allow the crust to cool slightly on the stovetop.

5. While the crust is cooling, make the filling. **Open** the packet of pudding, and **pour** it into a medium mixing bowl. **Add** milk and **stir** with a whisk for 2 minutes until thickened.

6. Peel the bananas. Use a table knife and a cutting board to **slice** them into ¼-inch rounds. Arrange the banana slices evenly across the bottom of the piecrust.

7. Use a rubber scraper to **scrape** the pudding into the piecrust to cover the bananas. **Spread** evenly.

8. **Chill** the pie for 1 hour or until ready to serve. Top with whipped topping, and enjoy!

TRY THIS!

To make a **chocolate cream pie**, leave out the banana slices. Use chocolate pudding instead of banana pudding. Before adding the pudding to the piecrust, mix 1 cup of whipped topping, such as Cool Whip, into the pudding.

makes 20 pies

preparation time: 25 minutes
baking time: 7 to 10 minutes per
cookie sheet

ingredients:

1 cup (2 sticks) unsalted butter
4 ounces cream cheese
¾ cup milk
1 tablespoon cider vinegar
1¾ cups flour
½ teaspoon salt
1 teaspoon baking powder
¼ teaspoon baking soda
2 teaspoons ground ginger
1¼ teaspoons cinnamon
1¼ teaspoons ground cloves
½ teaspoon allspice
¾ cup brown sugar
1 egg
½ cup molasses
1 teaspoon vanilla extract
1 (7-ounce) jar marshmallow creme

equipment:

2 cookie sheets
parchment paper
liquid measuring cup
measuring spoons
fork
2 medium mixing bowls
1 cup measuring cups—1 cup, ¼ cup
electric mixer
spatula
wire cooling rack
small mixing bowl
rubber scraper
waxed paper
air-tight containers with lids

Creamy Ginger Whoopie Pies

Whoopie pies are made by pressing a layer of creamy filling between two cakelike cookies. They make a great lunchbox treat.

1. **Remove** the butter and the cream cheese from the refrigerator so that they have time to soften.

2. **Place** 2 oven racks near the center of the oven. **Preheat** the oven to 350°F. **Place** parchment paper on 2 cookie sheets.

3. In a liquid measuring cup, **add** milk and cider vinegar. **Mix** with a fork. Set aside.

4. In a medium mixing bowl, **combine** flour, salt, baking powder, baking soda, ground ginger, cinnamon, ground cloves, and allspice. **Mix** well with the fork.

5. In another medium mixing bowl, **add** 1 stick of softened butter and brown sugar. (Be sure to pack the brown sugar tightly into the measuring cup before adding.) Use an electric mixer to **blend** until fluffy.

Turn the page for more Creamy Ginger Whoopie Pies

6. **Crack** the egg into the butter mixture and mix well. **Add** the molasses, and **mix** until well combined.

7. **Add** a third of the flour mixture to the butter mixture. **Mix** well with the electric mixer. Then **add** a third of the milk mixture and **mix** well. **Repeat** 2 more times, until all the flour and milk has been mixed into the butter mixture.

8. **Drop** the batter by rounded tablespoonfuls onto the prepared cookie sheets. Leave 2 inches between each spoonful.

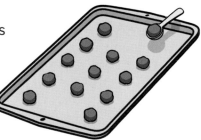

9. Use oven mitts to **place** the cookie sheets on the center racks in the oven. **Bake** for 7 to 10 minutes, or until firm to the touch. Use oven mitts to **remove** the pans from the oven. Use a spatula to **place** the cookies on the wire cooling rack. But do not stack the cookies—they will stick together!

10. **Repeat** steps 8 and 9 until you've used all the batter. Allow the cookies to cool completely.

11. While the cookies are cooling, make the filling. **Add** the second stick of softened butter and the cream cheese to a small mixing bowl. Use the electric mixer to **blend** until fluffy. **Add** the vanilla extract and the marshmallow creme. **Mix** well.

12. Use a rubber scraper to **spread** the filling on the flat bottom of one cooled cookie. **Place** the flat bottom of a second cooled cookie on top of the filling. Gently **press** the 2 cookies together. **Repeat** until all the cookies have been made into whoopie pies. Store in air-tight containers. Layer the pies between sheets of waxed paper to keep them from sticking.

TRY THIS!

If you don't have parchment paper, grease each cookie sheet with 1 tablespoon butter.

Use your favorite cake recipe to make the cookies. **Chocolate** or **coconut** cakes are tasty choices.

Flavor the filling with other extracts. Add ¼ teaspoon **peppermint** extract to the filling if you're making chocolate cookies. Or add ¼ teaspoon **almond** extract to the filling for coconut cake cookies.

makes 10 cream puffs

preparation time: 15 minutes
baking time: 35 to 40 minutes

ingredients:

1 cup water
½ cup (1 stick) unsalted
   butter
1 teaspoon sugar
¼ teaspoon salt
1 cup all-purpose flour
4 eggs
1 tablespoon coarse sugar
   (optional)
1 (13-ounce) can spray
   whipped cream

equipment:

2 cookie sheets
medium saucepan
liquid measuring cup
measuring spoons
wooden spoon
measuring cup—1 cup
tablespoon
serrated knife

Easy Cream Puffs

Cream puffs are amazingly easy to make. As they bake, air holes form in the dough. The holes are perfect for filling with sweet whipped cream. Mmm, mmm!

1. **Place** 2 oven racks near the center of the oven. Then **preheat** the oven to 450°F.

2. In a medium saucepan, **combine** the water, butter, sugar, and salt. Turn the burner under the saucepan on medium. Bring the mixture to a **boil**, stirring occasionally. Then turn off the burner.

3. **Add** flour to the saucepan. **Stir** briskly with a wooden spoon. Keep stirring until the mixture pulls away from the sides of the pan and sticks to the spoon. A ball should form around the spoon. If it doesn't, turn the burner on low. Stir for 3 to 5 more seconds. Then turn off the burner. Allow the mixture to cool slightly.

4. **Crack** the eggs into the saucepan one at a time. **Stir** well after adding each one.

5. **Scoop** a tablespoon of dough from the saucepan. **Drop** it onto an ungreased cookie sheet. Repeat with the rest of the dough, keeping each scoop 2 inches apart. If you'd like, **sprinkle** coarse sugar over the tops of the puffs.

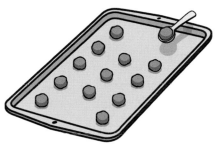

Turn the page for more Easy Cream Puffs

Easy Cream Puffs continued

6. Use oven mitts to **place** the cookie sheets on the center racks in the oven. **Bake** for 15 minutes. Then reduce heat to 350°F. **Bake** for 20 to 25 minutes more, or until the sides of the puffs are sturdy. Be careful not to overbake.

7. **Cool** the puffs for 15 minutes on the cookie sheets. Use a serrated knife to **cut** the top off each puff. **Fill** each puff with a squirt of whipped cream. Then **place** the top back on each puff and serve.

TRY THIS!

Place a teaspoon of your favorite jam into each puff before filling with whipped cream.

Fill each puff with store-bought **lemon curd**. Or fill with a thick, completely cooled **chocolate pudding**.

Sweet Strawberry Shortcake

Give this classic summertime treat a try. If you don't have time to make the cake, buy angel food cake from the bakery section at your local grocery store.

1. **Place** an oven rack in the center of the oven. **Preheat** the oven to 325°F. **Grease** 2 loaf pans with butter. Use a paper towel to spread the butter on the bottom, corners, and sides of each pan.

Turn the page for more Sweet Strawberry Shortcake

serves 4

preparation time: 20 minutes
baking time: 35 to 45 minutes

ingredients:

1 tablespoon butter
2 cups fresh strawberries
(16-ounce package)
⅓ cup sugar
2 teaspoons vanilla extract
1 (16-ounce) package angel
food cake mix
1¼ cups water
1 cup heavy cream
1 tablespoon powdered sugar
¼ teaspoon salt

equipment:

colander
cutting board
knife
2 medium mixing bowls
measuring cup—⅓ cup
measuring spoons
wooden spoon
liquid measuring cup
electric mixer
rubber scraper
2 (9-inch) loaf pans
table knife
wire cooling rack
serrated knife
4 dessert plates
ziplock bags
2 spoons

2. **Wash** the strawberries in a colander under cool water. Use the cutting board and the knife to **cut** around the stem of the fruit. Discard the stems, and cut the berries in half. **Place** the cut berries in a medium mixing bowl. **Sprinkle** with sugar and ½ teaspoon vanilla extract. **Stir** with a wooden spoon to coat the berries. Set aside.

3. In a medium mixing bowl, **combine** cake mix with water. **Mix** with an electric mixer for 1 minute on medium speed. Use a rubber scraper to **scrape** the cake batter into the 2 greased loaf pans. **Wash** the beaters and the mixing bowl. Then **place** them in the freezer to chill.

4. Use oven mitts to **place** the filled loaf pans on the center rack in the oven. **Bake** for 35 to 45 minutes, or until the top is golden brown and cracked. The top should feel very dry, not sticky.

5. Use oven mitts to **remove** the loaf pans from the oven. Immediately **turn** the loaf pans on their sides on a wire cooling rack.

6. When the cakes are completely cool, run a table knife between the cake and the sides of each pan. Then **tip** the pans upside down over the cooling rack to remove the cakes.

7. Remove the small mixing bowl and beaters from the freezer. **Measure** the heavy cream into the mixing bowl. **Mix** with an electric mixer until the mixture thickens and soft peaks begin to form. Turn off the mixer, and **add** 1½ teaspoons vanilla extract, powdered sugar, and salt. **Mix** for 30 seconds more, just to combine.

8. Slice the cake into 2-inch-thick slices with a serrated knife. **Place** a slice on 4 dessert plates. Put the extra slices in ziplock bags for later use. They will last for about 2 days unrefrigerated. Or you can freeze them for another time.

9. Mash the strawberries slightly with a fork. **Place** 2 spoonfuls over each slice of cake. **Top** each dessert with a spoonful of whipped cream. Serve immediately.

TRY THIS!

Thaw the extra frozen cake slices when you want more strawberry shortcake. While the cake thaws, follow step 2. Then follow step 9 and enjoy!

Use a mix of **raspberries** and **blueberries** instead of strawberries. Do not mash.

Top cakes with whipped topping or canned whipped cream instead of heavy whipping cream.

makes 16 squares

preparation time: 20 minutes
baking time: 1 hour

ingredients:

7 tablespoons unsalted butter,
   softened
5 medium apples
½ cup frozen cranberries
1 teaspoon apple pie spice
¾ cup brown sugar
¾ cup all-purpose flour,
   plus 2 tablespoons for
   topping
¼ teaspoon salt
½ cup old-fashioned oats
½ teaspoon baking powder
½ cup sugar

equipment:

9-inch square pan
colander
vegetable peeler
knife
cutting board
large mixing bowl
measuring spoons
measuring cups—½ cup,
   ¼ cup
wooden spoon
whisk
medium mixing bowl
fork
oven mitts
wire cooling rack

Apple Cranberry Crisp

This is the perfect fall dessert. It'll fill your house
with the sweet, warm smell of apple pie spice.

1. **Remove** the butter from the refrigerator
   so that it has time to soften.

2. **Place** an oven rack in the center of the oven.
   Preheat the oven to 375°F. **Grease** a baking pan
   with 1 tablespoon butter. Use a paper towel to spread
   the butter on the bottom, corners, and sides of the pan.

3. **Wash** the apples under cool water. **Wash** the
   cranberries in a colander under cool water.

4. **Peel** the apples with a sharp vegetable
   peeler. Then use a knife and a cutting
   board to chop each apple. First,
   cut the apple in half from
   top to bottom. Cut each
   half in half again from top
   to bottom. Then cut out and
   discard the stem and seeds.
   Chop into bite-size pieces. Chop
   enough to measure 5½ cups. Place
   in a large mixing bowl, and set aside.

5. On the cutting board, **chop** the frozen cranberries into chunks. **Add** to the large mixing bowl.

6. **Add** apple pie spice, brown sugar, 2 tablespoons flour, and salt to the large mixing bowl. (Be sure to pack the brown sugar tightly into the measuring cup before adding.) **Stir** with a wooden spoon to mix well. **Pour** the apple mixture into the greased baking pan. Use the wooden spoon to spread the mixture evenly in the bottom of the pan.

Turn the page for more Apple Cranberry Crisp

TRY THIS!

Make this crisp with other fruits. Rhubarb and strawberries or peaches with raspberries are nice combinations. Chop a total of 5½ cups of fruit.

Replace oats with chopped almonds or other nuts.

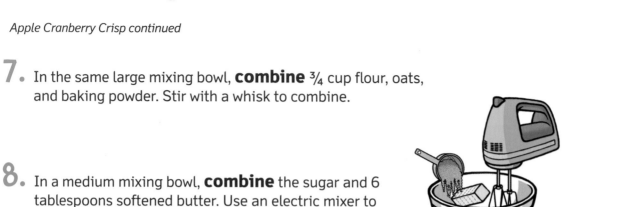

7. In the same large mixing bowl, **combine** ¾ cup flour, oats, and baking powder. Stir with a whisk to combine.

8. In a medium mixing bowl, **combine** the sugar and 6 tablespoons softened butter. Use an electric mixer to **blend** until fluffy.

9. **Add** the flour mixture to the butter mixture. Use a fork to **mix**. **Pour** the flour and butter mixture over the apples. Use a wooden spoon to **spread** the topping evenly over the fruit.

10. Use oven mitts to **place** the baking pan on the center rack in the oven. **Bake** for 1 hour, or until brown on top. Use oven mitts to **remove** the pan from the oven. Let the crisp **cool** on a wire cooling rack for at least 30 minutes before serving.

SPECIAL INGREDIENTS

apple pie spice: a blend of cinnamon, nutmeg, cloves, and cardamom spices. Apple pie spice is available in the baking aisle of most grocery stores.

cider vinegar: a vinegar made from apple cider. It can be found with the white vinegar in most grocery stores.

coarse sugar: coarsely ground sugar used to add a slightly sweet decoration to the top of baked treats. Look for it in the baking section of the grocery store.

graham cracker crust: a piecrust made from graham cracker crumbs. It is available in the baking aisle of the grocery store.

heavy cream: thick, creamy milk available as cream or heavy whipping cream in the dairy section of your grocery store.

marshmallow creme: a sweet, creamy spread made with egg whites, sugar, and vanilla flavoring. Jars of marshmallow creme can be found in the baking aisle of your grocery store.

oats: a type of grain that comes from the oat plant. Oats can be found in the cereal aisle of the grocery store.

puff pastry: sheets of ready-made dough available in the freezer section of your grocery store

vanilla extract: liquid vanilla flavor. You can find vanilla extract in the baking section of the grocery store. Most stores sell both pure vanilla extract and artificially flavored extract. Either type will work.

whipped topping: a creamy topping made mainly from whipped vegetable oil and sugar. Whipped toppings such as Cool Whip are located in the freezer section of the grocery store.

FURTHER READING AND WEBSITES

ChooseMyPlate
http://www.choosemyplate.gov
/children-over-five.html
Play a game about making healthy food choices or print out coloring pages about nutrition at this website.

Cleary, Brian P. Food Is CATegorical series. Minneapolis: Millbrook Press, 2011.
This seven-book illustrated series offers a fun introduction to the food groups and other important health information.

Nissenberg, Sandra. *The Everything Kids' Cookbook: From Mac 'n Cheese to Double Chocolate Chip Cookies—90 Recipes to Have Some Finger-Lickin' Fun.* Avon, MA: Adams Media, 2008.
This cookbook is a great source for recipes kids love to make, including many dessert recipes.

Recipes
http://www.sproutonline.com
/crafts-and-recipes/recipes
Find more fun and easy recipes for kids at this site.

Weil, Carolyn Beth. *Williams-Sonoma Kids in the Kitchen: Sweet Treats.* New York: Free Press, 2006.
This cookbook has fun dessert recipes that are easy for kids to make, including everything from ice cream sandwiches to cakes and lemon bars.

INDEX

You're the Chef
Metric Conversions

VOLUME

⅛ teaspoon	0.62 milliliters
¼ teaspoon	1.2 milliliters
½ teaspoon	2.5 milliliters
¾ teaspoon	3.7 milliliters
1 teaspoon	5 milliliters
½ tablespoon	7.4 milliliters
1 tablespoon	15 milliliters
⅛ cup	30 milliliters
¼ cup	59 milliliters
⅓ cup	79 milliliters
½ cup	118 milliliters
⅔ cup	158 milliliters
¾ cup	177 milliliters
1 cup	237 milliliters
2 quarts (8 cups)	1,893 milliliters
3 fluid ounces	89 milliliters
12 fluid ounces	355 milliliters
24 fluid ounces	710 milliliters

MASS (weight)

1 ounce	28 grams
3.4 ounces	96 grams
3.5 ounces	99 grams
4 ounces	113 grams
7 ounces	198 grams
8 ounces	227 grams
12 ounces	340 grams
14.5 ounces	411 grams
15 ounces	425 grams
15.25 ounces	432 grams
16 ounces (1 pound)	454 grams
17 ounces	482 grams
21 ounces	595 grams

TEMPERATURE

Fahrenheit	Celsius
170°	77°
185°	85°
250°	121°
325°	163°
350°	177°
375°	191°
400°	204°
425°	218°
450°	232°

LENGTH

¼ inch	0.6 centimeters
½ inch	1.27 centimeters
1 inch	2.5 centimeters
2 inches	5 centimeters
3 inches	7.6 centimeters
5 inches	13 centimeters
8 inches	20 centimeters
9 x 11 inches	23 x 28 centimeters
9 x 13 inches	23 x 33 centimeters